EDUCATION LIBRARY
UNIVERSITY OF KENTUCKY

State Flowers

DISTRICT OF COLUMBIA

American Beauty rose

ANNE OPHELIA DOWDEN

STATE FLOWERS

Illustrated by the Author

THOMAS Y. CROWELL · NEW YORK

J582.130
Dow

ACKNOWLEDGMENTS

For many years, I have been collecting the material in this book, and innumerable people have helped me with information and plant specimens. To all of them, I give sincere thanks. For special help with some of the transcripts of state laws, I am indebted to Mr. William Winship and to the staff of Audubon *magazine, where in 1970 this material appeared in different form.*

All plants are pictured at exactly ⅔ natural size.

Copyright © 1978 by Anne Ophelia Dowden.
All rights reserved. Except for use in a review,
the reproduction or utilization of this work in
any form or by any electronic, mechanical, or
other means, now known or hereafter invented,
including xerography, photocopying, and record-
ing, and in any information storage and retrieval
system is forbidden without the written permission
of the publisher. Published simultaneously in
Canada by Fitzhenry & Whiteside Limited, Toronto.
For information address Thomas Y. Crowell,
10 East 53 Street, New York, N. Y. 10022.
Manufactured in the United States of America

Library of Congress Cataloging in Publication Data
Dowden, Anne Ophelia Todd. State flowers.
SUMMARY: Presents a description of and background
information about each of the fifty state flowers.
1. State flowers—Juvenile literature. [1. State
flowers.   2. Flowers.   3. Emblems, State]   I. Title.
QK85.D68   1978   582.13'0973   78-51927
ISBN 0-690-01339-6   ISBN 0-690-03884-4 lib. bdg.
First Edition

Contents

Of State Flowers and Their Statutes

In 1892, when the whole United States was preparing for the first Chicago World's Fair, women's groups in three of our western states proposed to their legislatures that floral emblems be chosen to accompany the state exhibits. Oklahoma, then still a territory, quickly acted on the suggestion, and in January 1893, its mistletoe became our first legally designated floral emblem. A month later, Minnesota's legislature adopted the lady slipper; but Washington's two houses did not act, and its rhododendron, though elected by a state-wide women's vote, did not become official till many years later.

Another state, however, already had an unofficial flower. In 1890, the schoolchildren of New York had voted for the goldenrod as state emblem. A year later, they voted again, this time electing the rose, but their choice was not adopted by the legislature until 1955. Several other state-flower laws were enacted even more recently than that; but by 1968, floral emblems had been made official in all our fifty states and the District of Columbia.

In the following pages, these statutes are given verbatim, except for the occasional omission of some legal locutions. The states are presented alphabetically with the exception of a few cases in which two states have the same flower and are placed together. Any state not in its normal alphabetical position can be found in the Contents. Over the years, many of the statutes have been periodically reenacted, and some have been changed. Given here are, first, the dates of the original actions, and, second—when pertinent —the dates of the latest reenactments or verifications.

The statutes themselves are useful. Though some of them are brief and dull in their legal wording, others are poetic, giving us a glimpse of the feeling and thinking behind the choice of flower. At the very least, they let us know exactly what the legislators wanted, which is often misinterpreted because very few people have ever seen the actual wording of the laws.

Some of the resolutions designate a flower in general terms—Illinois' "native violet," for instance; others name a particular species, like Rhode Island's *Viola palmata*. Scientific names, however, have their pitfalls. Since the legislators were seldom botanists, they sometimes made mistakes with the Latin names of species, chiefly in the matter of spelling. And, to make things more difficult for them, some scientific names have been changed by botanists, who are constantly studying and reclassifying plants.

It would be interesting to know the stories behind all these floral selections, but only occasionally are the stories to be found in the statutes themselves. We know that many state flowers were chosen by vote of schoolchildren; others were recommended and lobbied for by garden clubs or patriotic groups, often with intense fervor. But who chose, from among many similar flowers, the species named by Nebraska or Wyoming? Why did some states change their minds? Who promoted Tennessee's iris in place of its original wild passionflower?

An appropriate state flower, one might think, would be a native plant, common, well loved, and handsome. But many of our floral emblems are not native. Nearly all American garden flowers came originally from Europe or Asia, including Indiana's peony and Ohio's carnation. So did all our commercial fruits, like Florida's orange. Even some of our wildflowers, like Vermont's clover, came here from abroad, escaped from cultivation, and "went native." All of them, however, are beautiful flowers, and they have been here a long time. If they have Old World origins, so also do most of the Americans who grow and cherish them.

CAMELLIA
Camellia japonica

Alabama

The camellia is hereby designated and named as the official state flower of Alabama.   *1959*

For 30 years or more, before the adoption of the camellia, Alabama's state flower was the goldenrod, chosen by its schoolchildren. The displacement of this beautiful native plant might possibly seem unfortunate, but only to one who has never seen Alabama's magnificent camellias.

The state lies in the center of the Camellia Belt, where this shrub thrives out-of-doors in a climate much like that of its native habitat in tropical or near-tropical Asia. Camellias were named for a Jesuit priest, G. J. Kamel, who traveled in Asia in the seventeenth century. Other explorers brought the plant to Europe, where by the late eighteenth century it was grown with enthusiasm, written about, and pictured. At nearly the same time, it reached the United States. There are about 80 species of camellia (including the tea plant), but few of them are grown in this country. Our hundreds of varieties are mostly hybrids based on only two species, *Camellia japonica* and *C. sasanqua*.

FORGET-ME-NOT
Myosotis alpestris

Alaska

AN ACT *Designating and declaring the forget-me-not to be the territorial and floral emblem of Alaska.*

A LITTLE FLOWER BLOSSOMS FORTH ON EVERY HILL AND DALE.

WHEREAS, . . . *Alaska has a wildflower which grows on every hill and in every valley; and,*

THE EMBLEM OF THE PIONEERS UPON THE RUGGED TRAIL;

WHEREAS, *this flower is emblematic of the quality of constancy, the dominant trait of the intrepid pioneers, who, . . . have opened for development a nation's treasure house; and,*

THE PIONEERS HAVE ASKED IT AND WE COULD DENY THEM NOT;

WHEREAS, *the Grand Igloo of the Pioneers of Alaska has indorsed this floral gem as the territorial flower of Alaska;*

SO IN THINKING OF AN EMBLEM FOR THIS EMPIRE OF THE NORTH WE WILL CHOOSE THIS AZURE FLOWER THAT THE GOLDEN DAYS BRING FORTH.

FOR WE WANT THEM TO REMEMBER THAT ALASKA CAME TO STAY, THO SHE SLEPT UNKNOWN FOR AGES AND AWAKENED IN A DAY. SO, ALTHO THEY SAY WE'RE LIVING IN THE LAND THAT GOD FORGOT, WE'LL RECALL ALASKA TO THEM WITH OUR BLUE FORGET-ME-NOT.

THEREFORE, *Be it enacted by the Legislature of the Territory of Alaska: Section 1*

That the wild forget-me-not is hereby made, designated, and declared to be the territorial flower and floral emblem of the Territory of Alaska.

SO THE EMBLEM OF ALASKA IS THE BLUE FORGET-ME-NOT.   *1917*

SAGUARO CACTUS
Carnegiea gigantea

Arizona

The pure white waxy flower of the cereus giganteus (giant cactus) or Saguaro shall be the state flower.   *1931, 1973*

The majestic saguaro cactus, which botanists now call *Carnegiea gigantea*, dominates the Arizona desert. Shaped like a huge candelabrum, it can grow almost 50 feet high and weigh seven tons. Much of its weight is due to water, taken up in great quantities during the short rainy season and stored for dry-season use in roots and stems that have a thick hard skin to prevent evaporation. Saguaro flowers are pollinated by bats and doves, as well as by the more usual bees, and they produce vast numbers of seeds. Millions of seeds reach the ground, but few find the right soil and enough moisture to sprout; and fewer still live to maturity since the plants grow only an inch a year. A large cactus is often 150 or 200 years old.

The saguaro's numbers are dwindling. Cattle and increasing dryness are partly responsible, but the greatest threat is the horde of thieves who dig up the precious young plants for sale to gardeners.

APPLE BLOSSOM
Pyrus malus

Arkansas

RESOLVED *by Both Houses of the General Assembly, That the "Apple Blossom" be declared the State floral emblem of Arkansas.* *1901*

Though Arkansas has native wild crabapples, its legislators were probably thinking of its cultivated orchards when they passed their resolution.

This commercial fruit is largely man's creation, the product of his meddling ever since Neolithic times. Our orchard trees are all descendants of an ancient Eurasian species. In the early Mediterranean world, gardeners learned to select natural variations and to propagate them, until by the first century after Christ, the Romans grew thirty-six good varieties. The Romans took their apples to England, and the English brought them to America. Through the centuries, the world has seen the development of perhaps 100,000 varieties, all propagated by grafting, because apple hybrids almost never come true from seed. Johnny Appleseed, who traveled across the country planting seeds, would have been very disappointed if he had been around when all his trees finally bore fruit.

GOLDEN POPPY
Eschscholtzia californica

California

The golden poppy (Eschscholtzia) is the official State flower.
1903, 1943

In California, valleys and fields and mountainsides are often blanketed with these glowing golden flowers, so brilliant that early Spaniards named the coast "Land of Fire." One hillside north of Pasadena is said to have served as a beacon for ships twenty-five miles at sea.

The plant was first described by the German poet and naturalist Adalbert von Chamiso, who in 1815 sailed around the world on a Russian ship, along with the zoologist J. F. Eschscholtz. As a gesture of friendship, he bestowed that ponderous scientific name on the slender and fragile poppy.

Of the many species of eschscholtzia, California's flower is probably the best known. It grows wild from southern California to the Columbia River, and it is the parent of most garden varieties. Very similar species are found as far east as Utah and New Mexico. Their juice is a mild narcotic, said to be used by the Indians to relieve toothache.

COLUMBINE
Aquilegia coerulea

Colorado

The white and lavender columbine is hereby made and declared to be the state flower of the state of Colorado.

1899, 1973

This graceful and elegant plant brightens the slopes of the Rockies from Montana to Mexico. In aspen groves or on open hillsides, it still grows in abundant masses, but it is seriously threatened by wanton picking and is therefore protected by law.

Many kinds of columbine grow wild in North Temperate regions around the world. A European species, once valued for medicine and magic, has been a cherished garden plant since the Middle Ages. It received the name columbine because its flowers resembled circles of little doves (*columbae* in Latin). Another bird inspired the genus name *Aquilegia*, which comes from the Latin *aquila*, eagle, presumably because the flower spurs looked like a bird's talons. These spurs, which hold the nectar, vary greatly in different species, but they all require a pollinator with a long tongue, like a moth or a hummingbird. Colorado's columbine is the parent of most long-spurred garden hybrids.

MOUNTAIN LAUREL
Kalmia latifolia

Connecticut

*The mountain laurel, Kalmia latifolia, shall be the state
flower.*   *1907, 1949*

Pennsylvania

*The mountain laurel (Kalmia Latifolia) is hereby adopted
as the State flower of Pennsylvania.*   *1933*

In Connecticut and Pennsylvania—in fact, all the way
from Canada to the Gulf of Mexico—this handsome
shrub fills the early summer woods with great drifts of
pink and white blossoms. The Swedish botanist Pehr
Kalm was more impressed by mountain laurel than by
any other plant during his exploration of America in
the 1750s. He introduced it to Europe and gave it his
name.

Even when the shrub is not in flower, the smooth
evergreen leaves are beautiful, though also deadly.
Cattle and grouse die when they are tempted to nibble
the young spring shoots, and it is said that Indians
drank a decoction of the leaves to commit suicide.
The wood, very hard and dense, is used for making
small objects like spoons and pipes, and the plant is
sometimes called spoonwood.

PEACH BLOSSOM
Prunus persica

Delaware

The Peach Blossom, as originally adopted as the floral emblem of the State of Delaware on May 9, 1895, shall be the official State Flower.   *1895, 1955*

Delaware was the fifth state to designate its emblem by legal action, and the flower it chose is beautiful, economically important, and celebrated in art and legend throughout the world.

Peaches are not native to North America, but have traveled two thirds of the way around the globe to get here. They apparently originated in the high forests of Central China, where small wild peaches still grow, and they have been cultivated in China since about 3000 B.C. By the time of Christ, they had made their way to Kashmir and Persia, and from there they traveled westward with the march of civilization. By the Middle Ages, peaches were grown all over Europe, and they came to the New World with the first explorers. The Spanish planted them in Mexico, the French in Louisiana, the English in Jamestown; and soon peaches were so much at home in America that some have been mistaken for true natives.

ORANGE BLOSSOM
Citrus sinensis

Florida

WHEREAS, *the State of Florida is universally known as the "Land of Flowers":*

THEREFORE, *Be it resolved by the House of Representatives, the Senate concurring: That the Orange Blossom be, and the same is hereby chosen and designated as the State Flower in and for the State of Florida.*   *1909*

More oranges are now grown in Florida than anywhere else in the world, but there were none at all in the western hemisphere until Columbus himself brought them to the Caribbean. Though Spain and Portugal had for centuries been famous for their fine oranges, the fruit originally came from southern China, where it was first described about 500 B.C. From Asia, it slowly migrated westward into the Mediterranean basin, to become the "golden apple" of Greek legend and an important delicacy on the tables of Romans and other early Europeans. At that time oranges were seldom eaten as a food, but used instead for seasoning and decoration. And they were a fruit of the aristocracy. Not until the twentieth century did oranges become available to everyone.

CHEROKEE ROSE
Rosa laevigata

Georgia

WHEREAS, *The Cherokee Rose, having its origin among the aborigines of the northern portion of the State of Georgia, is indigenous to its soil, and grows with equal luxuriance in every county of the State,*

BE IT THEREFORE *by the House of Representatives of Georgia, the Senate concurring, resolved, That, at the suggestion and request of the Georgia Federation of Women's Clubs, the Cherokee Rose be . . . the floral emblem of the State of Georgia.*   *1916*

If the Georgia legislators had been botanists, they would have known that this lovely rose is not indigenous to the soil of that state. It runs wild in the South, so vigorous and abundant as to appear native, but it is really an import from China. *Rosa laevigata* probably came here by way of England; at any rate, it reached England in 1757 and the United States shortly thereafter. Very quickly it became an important wild rose in the South and thus was soon associated with the Cherokee Indians, to the extent that a number of "ancient Indian legends" grew up around it. The large white—or rarely pink—flowers are borne on sturdy vines that often climb to the top of trees.

HIBISCUS

Hibiscus rosa-sinensis

Hawaii

RESOLVED *by the Legislature of the Territory of Hawaii that the flower known as Pua Aloalo (Hibiscus) shall be and is hereby adopted as the flower emblematic of the Territory and shall be known as the Flower Emblem of Hawaii.*   *1923*

This flower chosen in Territorial days is still the emblem of the state of Hawaii. Hibiscus is an outstanding plant there, with three species native to the Islands and thirty-three varieties brought from other countries. These, through horticultural crossing, have produced more than 5,000 varieties. Commonest of all is *Hibiscus rosa-sinensis*, which came from Asia. The red flowers of this hibiscus, when crushed, yield a dark purplish dye, used in India for blackening shoes, and the plant is sometimes called shoeflower. In China it was used for medicine, and in Polynesia it was a sacred flower.

The many species of hibiscus vary greatly: some are trees 17 feet tall; some are shrubs; and some are small herbaceous plants. They bloom almost the entire year, but individual flowers usually open in the morning and die by sunset.

MOCK ORANGE
Philadelphus lewisii

Idaho

*The Syringa (Philadelphus lewisii) is hereby designated and
declared to be the state flower of the state of Idaho.   1931*

Lewis's mock orange is very much an Idaho native.
It grows only in the extreme northwestern corner of
the United States, though it has many close relatives
in the East and South. Nearly all of them are sometimes called "syringa," which is incorrect, because
syringa is really the scientific name of the lilac. The
mock orange's Latin name apparently comes from
the Egyptian king Ptolemy Philadelphus—why, no-
body knows. The *lewisii* of our species honors Meriwether Lewis, the famous explorer who, with
William Clark, charted the Northwest and collected
many new plants.

The mock orange is one of our best-known garden
shrubs, and innumerable varieties have been developed, chiefly hybrids of *Philadelphus coronarius*. Most
mock oranges have a rich and delicious fragrance, and
the very sweet flowers, with their waxy white petals
and profusion of yellow stamens, strongly resemble
orange blossoms.

VIOLETS
Viola pedata
V. papilionacea

Illinois

. . . and that the native violet be, and the same hereby is recognized and declared to be the native State flower of the State of Illinois.   *1908*

New Jersey

BE IT RESOLVED *by the House of Assembly, the Senate concurring: That the violet be and the same is hereby adopted as the flower emblematic of the State of New Jersey.*   *1913*

Any violet can be the emblem of Illinois and New Jersey, since neither state designates a particular species. There are many kinds to choose from—28 species that grow in one or both of these states and range in color from purple to white to yellow. The wood violet, *Viola papilionacea,* with its heart-shaped leaves, is probably the commonest one in both places, but the lovely *Viola pedata* also grows widely in these areas. It is called birds-foot violet because of its deeply cleft leaves.

Illinois adopted its flower after a vote by its schoolchildren in 1907. Asked to choose among the violet, the wild rose, and the goldenrod, they elected the violet.

PEONY
Paeonia cultivar

Indiana

. . . *and the flower of the peony (Paeonie) is hereby adopted and designated as the official state flower of the State of Indiana.*   *1957*

Indiana's present law does not suggest the complicated and curious history that preceded it. In 1913, the legislature adopted the carnation as state emblem, and then, in 1923, replaced it with the flower of the tulip tree. This action was overturned in 1931, when the tulip tree was made state tree and the zinnia became state flower. And finally, in 1957, the zinnia in turn was displaced by the present floral emblem, the peony.

Peonies are Old World plants, named for Paeon, physician to the Homeric gods. The ancient Greeks believed that the plant was of divine origin—an emanation of the moon—and that it shone in the dark and drove away evil spirits. It was therefore held to be a cure for those afflictions obviously caused by evil spirits—epilepsy, nightmares, and mental illness—and for this purpose it was used until well into the nineteenth century.

WILD ROSE
Rosa blanda

Iowa

WHEREAS, *The Executive Council has authorized the wild rose of Iowa as one of the decorations on the silver service presented to the battleship Iowa, therefore be it Resolved by the Senate, the House concurring, That the wild rose shall be officially designated as the flower of this State.* 1897

North Dakota

The floral emblem of the state of North Dakota shall be the wild prairie rose, rosa blanda or arkansana. 1907, 1943

Iowa's wild rose can very well be the same *Rosa blanda* that symbolizes North Dakota, since this species grows from Newfoundland to Missouri. But there are a great many pink wild roses in this region, all so much alike that only a botanist can tell them apart.

The dainty blooms of all these roses produce small red fruits, or hips. Most hips are reasonably good to eat, and during World War II they were often gathered as a source of Vitamin C in areas where citrus fruit was scarce. They are sometimes made into preserves, but more often are left as a favorite food for birds and other animals.

EDUCATION LIBRARY
UNIVERSITY OF KENTUCKY

SUNFLOWER
Helianthus annuus

Kansas

WHEREAS, *Kansas has a native wild flower common through-out her borders, hardy and conspicuous, of definite, unvarying and striking shape, easily sketched, moulded, and carved, having armorial capacities, ideally adapted for artistic re-production, with its strong, distinct disk and its golden circle of clear glowing rays—a flower that a child can draw on a slate, a woman can work in silk, or a man can carve on stone or fashion in clay; and*

WHEREAS, *This flower has to all Kansans a historic symbolism which speaks of frontier days, winding trails, pathless prairies, and is full of the life and glory of the past, the pride of the present, and richly emblematic of the majesty of a golden future, and is a flower which has given Kansas the world-wide name, "the sunflower state":*

THEREFORE, *Be it enacted by the Legislature of the State of Kansas: That the helianthus or wild native sunflower is hereby made, designated and declared to be the state flower and floral emblem of the state of Kansas.*   *1903, 1923*

This bright and beautiful flower grows wild through-out the United States, but it is most at home on the prairies. It was very early brought into cultivation by the Indians, who grew a large-flowered type that ex-plorers carried back to Europe in the sixteenth century. Now sunflowers are grown all over the world, but especially in Russia, where today's mammoth garden varieties were developed.

GOLDENROD

Solidago gigantea

Kentucky

The goldenrod is the official state flower of Kentucky.

1926

Nebraska

RESOLVED, *that, the senate concurring, we, the Legislature of Nebraska hereby declare the flower commonly known as the "Golden Rod"* (Solidago Serotina) *to be the floral emblem of the state.*   *1895*

Nebraska was one of the first states to adopt a floral emblem, but Kentucky's official choice came rather late, after the trumpet-creeper had served unofficially for many years.

Solidago serotina is now known by botanists as *S. gigantea,* a fitting name for this fine goldenrod that grows tall and handsome in Kentucky and Nebraska. But both states have many species, and there are about 85 American goldenrods. They are often, wrongly, blamed for the hayfever that is in fact caused by ragweed's wind-blown pollen. Far from being a menace to health, goldenrod has a long tradition as a healing herb. Used first by the American Indians, it was later included in medical botany; and in Elizabethan times, quantities of the dried plant were sent to England's apothecary shops.

MAGNOLIA
Magnolia grandiflora

Louisiana

The magnolia shall be the state flower of the State of Louisiana.
1900

Mississippi

WHEREAS, *in the month of November, 1900, the school children of the State of Mississippi by an overwhelming margin selected the magnolia as the state flower of Mississippi; and*

WHEREAS, *since said time the magnolia has been generally recognized as the state flower of Mississippi but has never been officially designated as such by the Legislature;*

NOW, THEREFORE: *Be it enacted by the Legislature of the State of Mississippi: . . . That the flower or bloom of the magnolia or evergreen magnolia (Magnolia grandiflora L.) is hereby designated as the state flower of Mississippi.* 1952

This loveliest of magnolias is truly a plant of the American South, though it is widely cultivated in other parts of the world. All present-day magnolias are native in tropical or near-tropical regions. There are about 85 species, but they are only a small remnant of the great magnolia forests that, in preglacial times, spread across Europe and America as far north as the Arctic Circle.

PINE CONE
Pinus strobus

Maine

RESOLVED, *That the Pine Cone and Tassel is hereby declared to be the floral emblem for Maine, in the National Garland of flowers.*   *1895, 1959*

Pines are almost exclusively trees of the northern hemisphere, especially of its temperate and frigid zones. In New England forests, the white pine is supreme—a quick-growing, handsome tree. In its young years it is pyramidal; in old age, broad, irregular, and picturesque. Its "flowers" are small male or female cones. The female cones are prettily tinged with pink, but they grow so high on the branch tips of tall trees that they are seldom visible. When the male cones release their pollen to the wind, however, the cloud of yellow dust leaves no doubt that the pine trees are in bloom. Once pollinated, the little female cones ripen slowly for two years before they are large enough to split and shed their winged seeds.

White-pine wood makes beautiful lumber, with few big knots. It was also valued for ship masts, and the tree was introduced into England and cultivated chiefly for that purpose.

BLACK-EYED SUSAN
Rudbeckia hirta

Maryland

His Excellency, the Governor of Maryland, is hereby empowered and directed to declare by proclamation on the first day of June, in the year 1918, the Rudbeckia hirta or black-eyed Susan as the floral emblem of the State of Maryland.
1918, 1951

The black-eyed Susan was probably chosen as Maryland's flower because, like the oriole, it carries Lord Baltimore's colors—black and orange. It is not a native of the state, but an immigrant from the western prairies, where it invaded sunny pastures and was carried eastward in bundles of hay. This is a reversal of the usual movement of American wild plants, which have commonly traveled westward, following the white man's migrations. Now the black-eyed Susan flourishes from May to September in dry fields and other open places all the way from the Rockies to the Atlantic.

Black-eyed Susans belong to the same family as sunflowers and daisies—the Composites. Each flower head is composed of hundreds of tiny florets—florets purple-brown and tubular in the central disk, orange and strap-shaped in the surrounding rays.

MAYFLOWER

Epigaea repens

Massachusetts

*The mayflower (epigaea repens) shall be the flower or
floral emblem of the commonwealth. . . .   1918, 1953*

This law goes on to state the penalties to be imposed
on anyone who pulls up the plant, penalties especially
severe "if a person does any of the aforesaid acts while
in disguise or secretly in the nighttime." Now the
mayflower or trailing arbutus is on the national list of
Protected Wild Plants, and federal authority backs up
the quaint state law.

Mayflower grows from Newfoundland to Florida
and west to Kentucky, but it is chiefly associated with
New England. There it has been the beloved herald
of spring ever since the Pilgrims first found its
deliciously fragrant flowers emerging from its winter-
worn leaves. One wonders why they called it "mayflower," because it usually blooms in March or April,
and in England mayflower was the hawthorn tree,
long used in pagan May Day ceremonies. The Pilgrims did not prophetically choose to travel in a ship
called *Mayflower*; it was an English ship named for
the English hawthorn.

WILD CRABAPPLE

Pyrus coronaria

Michigan

WHEREAS, *A refined sentiment seems to call for the adoption of a state flower; and*

WHEREAS, *Our blossoming apple trees add much to the beauty of our landscape, and Michigan apples have gained a world-wide reputation; and*

WHEREAS, *At least one of the most fragrant and beautiful flowered species of apple, the pyrus coronaria, is native to our state;*

THEREFORE *Resolved by the Senate and House of Representatives of the State of Michigan, That the apple blossom be . . . the state flower of the state of Michigan.*   *1897, 1948*

Michigan orchards unquestionably add much to the beauty of the landscape, and so also does this lovely wild crabapple. It blooms late in the spring, so wreathed with spicy-fragrant flowers that it amply earns both its common name, garland crab, and its scientific *Pyrus coronaria* (coronaria means "like a crown").

This American native is often an angular, wide-branched tree, at home by roadsides, though not suitable for gardens. Domestication does not improve its hard little yellow-green apples, but they have a delightful fragrance, and the early settlers gathered them to make an excellent jelly.

LADY SLIPPER
Cypripedium reginae

Minnesota

The pink and white lady slipper, Cypripedium reginae, is adopted as the official flower of the state of Minnesota.

1893, 1969

The very first legally designated state flowers were adopted almost simultaneously by Minnesota and Oklahoma. In 1892, when all the states were preparing exhibits for the Chicago World's Fair, the Ladies Auxiliary of Minnesota's Fair Commission asked the legislature to approve their choice of the lady slipper to represent the state. A bill was quickly passed, in February 1893—just a month after similar action in Oklahoma.

But for a long time there was confusion about the exact identity of the flower. Unofficially, the pink lady slipper, *Cypripedium acaule*, had been considered the state emblem; but for some reason, the yellow lady slipper, *C. calceolus*, was named in the 1893 law. Later, someone decided—wrongly—that the yellow lady slipper did not grow in Minnesota. And so, in 1902, the legislature reworded the law and finally designated the most beautiful species of all, *C. reginae*, the slipper of the queen.

HAWTHORN
Crataegus mollis

Missouri

The hawthorn, the blossom of the tree commonly called the "red haw" or "wild haw" and scientifically designated as "crataegus," is declared to be the floral emblem of Missouri and the state department of agriculture shall recognize it as such and encourage its cultivation on account of the beauty of its flower, fruit, and foliage.   *1923, 1957*

When Missouri adopted a state flower, the daisy was a popular first choice, but because of its European origin, it was rejected in favor of the native wild hawthorn. Some hawthorns also have European origins (and long histories of folklore and legend), but they are different hawthorns from ours—a very few species in Europe as compared to the more than 100 in North America. Two of ours are called red haw, *Crataegus mollis* and *C. crus-galli*. Both of them are handsome trees in all seasons, attracting birds with their dense foliage and edible fruits; both have long, sharp thorns.

The red haw was important to Missouri pioneers, who made jelly from its fruit and valued its hard, fine-grained wood for fuel and for making small objects like boxes, combs, and shuttles.

BITTERROOT
Lewisia rediviva

Montana

The flower known as lewisia rediviva (bitterroot) shall be the floral emblem of the state of Montana.   *1895, 1947*

In 1804–1806, the famous Lewis and Clark Expedition explored the northwestern part of the United States. Its two leaders collected many plants, which were given to the botanist Frederick Pursh for identification. Six years later, among the dried and pressed specimens, one root seemed to have signs of life; and when planted, it revived and grew. Pursh called this new plant *Lewisia rediviva*, commemorating both its remarkable resurrection and its discoverer, Meriwether Lewis.

Lewisia's common name is bitterroot, and in the region where the plant grows plentifully, it has given the name to mountains, a river, and a valley. Indians ate the starchy roots in the spring, when the bitter bark was easily peeled off. There are a number of lewisia species, chiefly in the northern Cascade and Rocky Mountains. They are members of the Portulaca family, related to garden portulacas and to the nefarious weed purslane.

SAGEBRUSH
Artemisia tridentata

Nevada

The shrub known as sagebrush (Artemisia tridentata or trifida) is hereby designated as the official state emblem of the state of Nevada.   *1959*

Sagebrush is one of the dominant shrubs in the Great Basin between the Rockies and the Sierras, and pioneer farmers knew that wherever it grew, alfalfa could, with irrigation, also be grown. In hazy gray masses, it softens the harsh landscape. Its grayish foliage, pungent in smell and sharp in taste, and its tiny wind-pollinated flowers are typical of the whole *Artemisia* genus.

There are about 200 species of artemisia, most of them growing in the semidesert regions of the world. The grayness of their foliage is due to fine, often velvety, hairs that cover the plant and help protect it from strong sun. The sharp taste probably discourages browsing animals, but it greatly interests man, and many of these plants are important seasonings and drugs. Tarragon, mugwort, and wormwood are all flavoring herbs—the last an ingredient in absinthe and vermouth—and southernwood keeps moths away from woolens.

LILAC
Syringa vulgaris

New Hampshire

The purple lilac, Syringa Vulgaris, is the state flower of New Hampshire.   *1919*

In New Hampshire, as elsewhere, May belongs to lilacs as June belongs to roses. And among all the modern lilacs blooming there each spring, not one surpasses the old favorite that has traditionally grown at the door of every New England farmhouse. Brought to America by the early colonists, this hardy shrub flourished and, with its delicious fragrance, broadcast memories of England to the homesick exiles.

The common lilac originated in the Balkan peninsula, and during the sixteenth century its cultivation spread rapidly all over Europe. It reached England at the time of Henry VIII and became an important garden plant there, along wth the Persian lilac, *Syringa persica*, which arrived a century later. One or the other of these lilacs shares in the ancestry of nearly all our horticultural varieties; but there are also many other species, mostly from the temperate parts of Asia, and some of them are now grown in gardens.

53

YUCCA

Yucca elata

New Mexico

WHEREAS, *New Mexico is in need of a distinctive official flower, and*

WHEREAS, *the First State Federation of Women's Clubs recommended the Yucca flower as such official flower, and*

WHEREAS, *the majority of the school children of the state also chose the Yucca as the state flower,*

NOW, THEREFORE, *Be It Enacted by the Legislature of the State of New Mexico: . . . The Yucca flower is hereby adopted as the official flower of the State of New Mexico.*   *1927*

The many species of yucca probably rank next to cacti as the most familiar plants of the southwestern United States. They are all New World natives, though a few have been cultivated in Europe for centuries. Botanically, they are shrubs; some grow to tree proportions, but in many species, the woody stem is below ground and not visible. All yuccas have lovely clusters of creamy-white flowers above dense masses of leaves so stiff and pointed as to suggest the common names Adam's needle and Spanish bayonet. Another name is soapweed, because the Indians used yucca root as soap. Other parts of the plant provided fibers for baskets and cloth.

WILD ROSE
Rosa carolina

New York

The rose shall be the official flower of the state in any color or combination of colors common to it. 1955

New York's rose waited a long time for official recognition—from 1891 till 1955. In 1890, this state was first in the country to choose a floral emblem, when its schoolchildren voted for the goldenrod. Then, the following year, they voted again and elected the rose, which served as New York's unofficial emblem until it finally received legal sanction. This flower can be any rose from field, florist, or garden; but a native wild species seems most appropriate, and *Rosa carolina* is one of the state's commonest and best-known wildflowers.

Similar wild roses grow throughout the northern hemisphere, and one of them, probably in Asia Minor, was the long-ago ancestor of all today's garden beauties. By Roman times, double (or many-petaled) roses were widely cultivated, and the first steps had been taken in the infinitely complicated process of crossing and recrossing that eventually led to the big, lush roses of today.

North Carolina

The Dogwood is hereby adopted as the official flower of the State of North Carolina. 1941

Virginia

The flower commonly known as American Dogwood (Cornus florida) is declared to be the floral emblem of the Commonwealth. 1918, 1966

For many years, North Carolinians regarded the daisy as their state flower, and Virginians generally accepted the Virginia creeper. But when their legislatures finally acted to adopt official emblems, both chose the flowering dogwood.

Many kinds of dogwood grow in the United States and Europe. In this species, the clusters of tiny yellowish flowers, common to all dogwoods, are surrounded by large white or pink bracts that look like petals. The scientific name *Cornus* comes from the Latin *cornu*, meaning horn, referring to the hardness of the wood. In parts of England, the tree is called skewerwood, and the name by which we know it, dagwood or dogwood, probably comes from the Old English *dagge*, a sharp-pointed object.

CARNATION
Dianthus caryophyllus

Ohio

The scarlet carnation is hereby adopted as the state flower as a token of love and reverence for the memory of William McKinley.   *1904, 1953*

Like President McKinley, most Americans are fond of the carnation, but it is not one of our native flowers. It came to us from Europe, where from the Middle Ages to the nineteenth century, only the rose was more beloved. Clove-gilliflowers, as early carnations were called, originated in central and southern Europe and were grown in monastery gardens for medicine and flavoring (hence one curious name, sops-in-wine). Norman monks brought them to England in Chaucer's time, and from then on they grew in every garden, valued as herbs but also for "pleasure of sight and smell." During the reign of Elizabeth I, a vast number of new varieties appeared, with double flowers, new colors, and striking striped and spotted patterns.

The crimson gilliflower, because of its strong clove scent, was a favorite, and its "carnation" color (from the Latin *carnis*, meaning meat) became the name for this kind of gilliflower.

MISTLETOE
Phoradendron flavescens

Oklahoma

The mistletoe shall be the floral emblem of the state.

1893, 1910

Oklahoma was still a territory when, in 1892, it was invited to participate in the Chicago World's Fair. In preparing this exhibit, women of the territory felt that they needed a floral emblem, and they petitioned the legislature, suggesting that the mistletoe be legally adopted. In January 1893, a bill to that effect was passed, beating Minnesota's state-flower bill by a month and making Oklahoma's mistletoe the first of all our officially designated floral emblems.

Mistletoe has fascinated mankind since primitive times. It is a parasitic plant that lives on the branches of trees and sends roots through the bark to get its food. Tiny flowers, scarcely visible, produce the clusters of translucent white berries. Both American mistletoe and its European cousin have been important in folk medicine. But in ancient Europe, mistletoe was also a magic herb—a symbol of purity and strength and, worn as an amulet, a protection against illnesses, demons, and disasters.

OREGON GRAPE
Mahonia aquifolium

Oregon

BE IT RESOLVED *by the senate, the house of representatives con-*
curring, That the Oregon grape (Berberis Aquifolium) be
and is hereby accepted as the Oregon state flower.   *1899*

Oregon grape, one of the small number of state flowers
made official before the turn of the century, was
chosen by the women's clubs of Portland and adopted
as the result of their petition to the legislature.

This handsome shrub, which most botanists now
put into the genus *Mahonia* rather than *Berberis*, belongs to the foothills and mountain slopes of Oregon,
Washington, and British Columbia. Many of the 100
or so species of mahonia are decorative plants, and
many, including Oregon grape, are grown in gardens
all over the United States and Europe. This plant is a
large shrub, with evergreen hollylike leaves that give
it the alternate name "holly grape," as well as its Latin
aquifolium (meaning sharp-leaved). Its masses of yellow flowers are followed by clusters of blue fruits that
look like blueberries and make delicious jelly.

VIOLETS
Viola palmata
V. papilionacea

Rhode Island

The flower commonly known as the "violet" (viola palmata) is hereby designated as the state flower for the state of Rhode Island. 1968

Wisconsin

The Wisconsin state flower is the wood violet (viola papilionacea). 1949, 1972

In both Rhode Island and Wisconsin, violets were chosen long ago by the schoolchildren and then not adopted by the legislature until much later. In 1909, Wisconsin's children nominated several wildflowers—violet, wild rose, trailing arbutus, and white water lily. On Arbor Day of that year, they voted and elected the violet, but the legislature did not legalize their choice until 1949. Rhode Island's children made their selection even earlier—in 1897—and the lawmakers delayed even longer—till 1968. These statutes designate very definite violets—two species that grow widely in eastern United States and that are similar except for *Viola palmata's* cleft leaves.

YELLOW JESSAMINE
Gelsemium sempervirens

South Carolina

The adoption of the Yellow Jessamine as the State Flower was the unanimous selection of the Engrossing Department of the General Assembly and the great majority of the ladies of the State who expressed a preference, and fervent interest has been manifested by many loyal and devoted citizens who revere our State and it is their supreme desire that her pure symbol should be the Yellow Jessamine, and we would recommend the Yellow Jessamine for the following reasons: (1) It is indigenous to every nook and corner of the State. (2) It is the first premonitor of coming spring. (3) Its fragrance greets us first in the woodland and its delicate flower suggests the pureness of gold. (4) Its perpetual return out of the dead winter suggests the lesson of constancy in, loyalty to, and patriotism in the service of the State.

THEREFORE, *we respectfully recommend that the Yellow Jessamine be adopted as the State Flower of South Carolina.*

1924

This report was adopted, and it appears to be the only official action in regard to South Carolina's state emblem. The lovely vine is often called "Carolina jessamine," though it grows throughout the South from Virginia to Texas. Its vigorous stems climb high into the trees to drape them with garlands of fragrant blossoms, and its roots produce the poisonous drug gelsemium.

69

PASQUEFLOWER
Anemone patens

South Dakota

The floral emblem of this state shall be the American pasque flower (Pulsatilla hirsutissima), the anemone or Mayflower, with the motto, "I lead."   *1903*

The pasqueflower does indeed lead, appearing so early in the spring that one wonders how it pushes through the frozen earth, and even through the snow. The flowers, protected from weather by their dense silvery fur, bloom before the leaves appear. These come later; deeply cut and hairy, they stand on tall stems along with the feathery seed heads. A very similar European species is commonly grown in rock gardens.

There has been great disagreement about the correct scientific name for this plant, but most botanists now call it *Anemone patens*. Pasqueflower means "Easter flower," probably because of the time of its bloom, though a green dye made from the flowers was sometimes used to color Easter eggs. Pasqueflowers have a strong acrid taste, and cows and horses will not eat them. The whole plant produces pulsatilla, at one time an official drug.

IRISES
Iris cultivar
I. pseudacorus

Tennessee

WHEREAS, *The State of Tennessee has never adopted a State Flower; and*

WHEREAS, *The Iris is one of the most beautiful and one of the most popular flowers in the State, its profusion and beauty attracting many visitors to the State,*
NOW, THEREFORE, *be it resolved . . . That the Iris be adopted as the State Flower of Tennessee.* 1933

In 1919, Tennessee's schoolchildren voted for the native wild passionflower or maypop, and for many years it was the unofficial floral emblem of the state. However, when legislative action finally came, the iris was adopted instead.

There is no way of knowing what particular iris, if any, the legislators had in mind, and Tennessee's flower can be either a garden variety or a wild species. Our hundreds of garden irises, now available in every conceivable color, are complicated hybrids; but the big bearded ones are all to some extent descended from a European plant—the so-called German iris, which has a deep violet flower with a yellow beard. The wild yellow iris, *I. pseudacorus*, is common in watery places throughout the eastern United States, but it, too, came here from Europe.

73

BLUEBONNET
Lupinus subcarnosus

Texas

WHEREAS, *the National Society of Colonial Dames of America in Texas have requested of the Legislature that it adopt the lupinus subcarnosus (generally known as buffalo clover or blue bonnet) as the State Flower,*

THEREFORE *Be it resolved by the Senate of the State of Texas, the House of Representatives concurring, that the lupinus subcarnosus . . . be the State flower of Texas.* 1901

Great fields of bluebonnets mirror the sky in all parts of Texas. Of the four native species, the largest and handsomest is *Lupinus texensis*, which most people mistakenly regard as the emblem of the state. In reality, the flower designated by the legislature at the request of the Colonial Dames of America is *L. subcarnosus*, a charming little plant, but one that grows only in a small corner of Texas.

There are 200 species of *Lupinus*, most native in America, but a few in southern Europe, where some kinds have been grown for centuries. They all bring nitrogen to poor soils, contradicting their scientific name: *Lupinus* comes from *lupus*, or wolf, because the plant was thought to eat up the soil.

75

SEGO LILY
Calochortus nuttallii

Utah

The sego lily is hereby selected as and declared to be the Utah state flower.   *1911, 1943*

In 1911, the children of Utah were called upon to select a wildflower for their state emblem. They chose the sego lily because its bulbs had saved the pioneers from starvation when they ran out of provisions in the early spring of 1848. The plant is thus a symbol of life and hope for all Mormons.

It is also one of the loveliest of western wildflowers, an elegant plant with large, beautifully patterned blossoms that suggest butterflies. The Spanish word for butterfly, *mariposa*, is the common name for many species of calochortus, and we have mariposa lilies, mariposa tulips, and butterfly tulips. Sego is an Indian name; and the scientific *Calochortus* comes from the Greek *calo*, beautiful, and *chortus*, grass, referring to the narrow leaves. There are about 60 species of calochortus, mostly west of the Rockies, with colors that range from white through yellow, orange, and pink to lavender.

77

RED CLOVER
Trifolium pratense

Vermont

The state flower shall be the red clover.   *1894, 1947*

Red clover is an ideal flower for a dairy region, and Vermont adopted it very early, the third state to act officially on a floral emblem. This clover is cultivated as a forage plant in all temperate parts of the world, and nearly everywhere it has also escaped to grow wild in sunny places. With its rich store of nectar, it is the delight of butterflies and bumblebees, which are its chief pollinators.

Red clover is by far the most important—and probably the best loved—of the world's 300 species of clover. Until recently, its flowers were an official medicine; but the whole plant—especially a rare "four-leafed clover"—was also considered magical: a symbol of hope, good fortune, and protection against witches. The name clover comes from the Anglo-Saxon *cloefre*, meaning club (the source of the design on our playing cards); and the scientific name, *Trifolium*, comes from *tres*, three, and *folium*, leaf.

79

WILD RHODODENDRON
Rhododendron macrophyllum

Washington

The native evergreen species, Rhododendron macrophyllum, is hereby designated as the official flower of the state of Washington.   *1949, 1959*

Washington's rhododendron came very close to being our first officially adopted state flower. When all the states were preparing exhibits for the 1892 Chicago World's Fair, Washington—along with Oklahoma and Minnesota—became interested in a floral emblem. In Washington, as elsewhere, the emblem was chosen by women, but only after an historic "War of the Flowers," waged by the followers of two indomitable ladies, one favoring rhododendron, the other, clover. After a campaign equal to the hottest political battle, a vote by the women of the state elected the rhododendron. The state senate promptly acted to confirm the choice—in February 1893—but the lower house did not. Only in 1949 did both houses of the legislature adopt the rhododendron, and even then they were uncertain about the species. In 1959 the law was finally reworded in its present form.

BIG LAUREL
Rhododendron maximum

West Virginia

WHEREAS, *Our present chief executive, the governor of the State, and his immediate predecessor, have each recommended the big laurel, or rhododendron, and the pupils of the public schools of the State . . . have voted for this flower;*

THEREFORE, *be it Resolved by the Legislature of West Virginia: That said rhododendron, or big laurel, be and it is hereby designated as the official State flower, to be used as such at all proper times and places.* 1903

This fine American shrub is usually called laurel in West Virginia, or sometimes rose bay. "Rhododendron" comes from two Greek words meaning "rose" and "tree."

West Virginia's rhododendron is an evergreen shrub that grows as far north as Nova Scotia, but is most abundant in the Appalachians and down into Georgia and Alabama. In early summer, it covers whole mountainsides with masses of bloom, usually white or pink-tinted, but occasionally lavender. Sometimes the plant is a low shrub, sometimes it towers 30 feet among the trees; and its wood is among the hardest and strongest that grows.

INDIAN PAINTBRUSH
Castilleja linariaefolia

Wyoming

The castillija linariaefolia, commonly called "the Indian paint brush," is hereby made and declared to be the state flower of the State of Wyoming.   *1917, 1945*

In Wyoming, as in all the West, "Indian paintbrush" is always a flower of the genus *Castilleja*. This is confusing to Easterners, who use the name for several quite different plants. Western castillejas are sometimes also called "painted cup," but the brilliant flowers really look like brushes dipped in intense color—or perhaps like flames.

About 100 kinds of castilleja grow in the Rocky Mountains, the Sierras, and the sagebrush regions of the West; and one kind grows in the East. Their conspicuous color, ranging in the various species from yellow, through orange and vermilion, to maroon, is all in the brilliant bracts and sepals that surround the true flowers. These flowers are merely slender yellow-green tubes, from which the stamens and pistils barely protrude. Their elongated shape and showy bracts are the delight of hummingbirds, their chief pollinators.

85

Index of Plants

UNIVERSITY OF KENTUCKY

EDUCATION LIBRARY
UNIVERSITY OF KENTUCKY